Fern Green

RECIPES FOR SMOOTHIES, JUICES,
NUT MILKS, AND TONICS TO DETOX, LOSE WEIGHT,
AND PROMOTE WHOLE-BODY HEALTH

TEN SPEED PRESS
Berkeley

CONTENTS

INTRODUCTION

These days, we seem to have a better understanding of how to control disease and the aging process. We know that it matters what we put into our bodies—we recognize the benefits that can be achieved by eating well, how it affects our energy levels, and how we feel about ourselves. Eating healthily gives us a positive outlook on life in general.

We also often hear that cooking can kill healthy enzymes and damage nutrients found in foods, and so we're looking for quick and easy ways to eat raw food.

What a great way to eat all those raw fruits and vegetables in your kitchen: take a handful of spinach, add an apple or two, throw them into your blender or juicer, and away you go—a fun-packed, nutrient-rich green drink! You would have to eat a lot of spinach in a salad to get the same amount of nutrients that you can by juicing.

This book will offer you helpful hints and fantastic recipe ideas to set you up on green drinks for life. Whether you want to lose weight, fight fatigue, combat disease, or just be healthier, adding green drinks into your diet will slowly transform your health for the better.

Top six green smoothie benefits

Smoothies can:

1. Cleanse and detox your body, as well as balance acid and alkaline levels, helping to prevent disease and heal existing health problems.

2. Help you to replace your caffeine fix with a natural energy boost.

3. Benefit kids who perhaps are not that keen on vegetables—you can hide the vegetables in with their favorite fruits.

4. Give you energy from the antioxidants and phytochemicals present.

5. Provide for a healthy snack or a meal replacement.

6. Help purify your blood because they are packed full of vitamins, enzymes, and chlorophyll.

A smoothie or a juice?

Smoothies and juices are both very good for you, and which you choose to drink is a matter of personal preference. Both are highly nutritious and use raw ingredients, but to make a smoothie, you use a blender, and to make a juice, you use a juicer (see page 9 for advice on equipment).

If you put some fruit and vegetables in your juicer, a great drink full of vitamins and minerals will pour out—one that you can drink quickly and will no doubt give you an energy boost, because all the nutrients will enter your bloodstream in a matter of minutes. Juicing is the quickest way of getting healthy greens into your body. The pulp that is left in the juicer (which it's best to empty and clean out right away) is where the fiber is. Fiber slows down the absorption of nutrients, which then release slowly into your system.

When you make smoothies, this pulp is whizzed in a blender and broken down into a thick liquid. You can adjust the consistency to your liking by adding water to make it more digestible. Smoothies contain fiber which is important to help the body eliminate waste, as it cleans your digestive tract and colon. It's recommended that you sip smoothies; drinking them too fast can cause bloating.

Having just one juice and one smoothie a day can yield incredible results for your body—just try it!

Green ingredients

When you begin mixing fruits and vegetables, it can be hard to get used to the "green taste." There is nothing wrong with this—you will find that you may need to experiment at the beginning as you might crave more fruit (that is, more sweetness). Most of the recipes in this book are roughly 60 percent vegetable to 40 percent fruit, and sometimes contain even less fruit.

Do remember to rotate the greens that you use in your smoothies and juices, as variety is key to supplying all those different nutrients to your body. It also keeps your taste buds interested!

EQUIPMENT

Blenders

Blenders can be useful tools in the kitchen because not only do they make smoothies, but they can also help make other delicious things such as soups and sauces. For these benefits alone, a powerful blender is a very good investment.

You will need to look for one preferably around 1,000 watts, with high revolutions per minute (RPM) and an advanced cutting action. This will create the smoothest of smoothies, which will ensure easy drinking.

Blenders at the low end of the market tend to burn out quickly, especially if used on a regular basis. You will need to set these blenders on a low speed to start, then increase it to blend all the ingredients completely.

Juicers

These days, there are many juicer models on the market that are easier to clean than the early models. Cleaning seems to be an important point—if it's too hard, it puts some people off juicing. Juicers vary widely in price and come in a variety of styles. The centrifugal juicer, which is relatively cheap, works at a high speed and juices very quickly. Other styles include masticating juicers or twin-gear ones. These juice a lot more slowly, which reduces the oxidation time of the juice—so you can keep it in the refrigerator for longer before it spoils.

Basil

Bok choy

Cabbage

Broccoli

SUPER GREENS

Greens have many benefits and are full of fantastic nutrients. We all try to include them in our diets, but it can be hard to eat them in large enough quantities that our bodies can make the most of these benefits. Juicing and blending these vegetables makes it easier to consume larger quantities than you would if you were eating them.

Also, all these leafy greens have cell walls composed mainly of cellulose, which is difficult for the body to break down. Juicing or blending these leafy greens makes the nutrients easier to absorb, thus increasing their uptake.

Basil

This popular herb is rich in nutrients necessary for cardiovascular health. It is often used as a natural anti-inflammatory and an inhibitor of bacterial growth, as it targets toxins affecting skin and hair. It can be great for those with inflammatory bowel conditions and arthritis. It's also a good source of vitamin K and contains iron, calcium, and vitamin A.

Cabbage

A great source of vitamins K and C, cabbages come in all sorts of shapes, sizes, and colors. Don't forget the brussels sprout comes under this category—it's just a tiny version of a cabbage. Cabbage juice can help prevent or cure stomach ulcers because of its fantastic anti-inflammatory properties.

Bok choy

Bok choy is a leafy Chinese cabbage, one of those cancer-fighting cruciferous greens. It contains a very high amount of vitamin K— almost half your recommended daily amount. It is a very light, leafy cabbage, easy to pack in your blender. It's also a good source of antioxidants and beta-carotene, which is good for your eyes.

Broccoli

The king vegetable of the cruciferous family, broccoli fights cancer, diabetes, Alzheimer's, heart disease, arthritis, and more. It contains vitamins C, K, and A as well as folate and fiber. The green florets can thicken up your smoothies, so you may need to add extra water, but remember you can use the stems too.

Green pepper

Celery

Kale

Chard

Dandelion greens

Cilantro

Celery

Celery has cooling properties that help maintain normal body temperature. It contains minerals that regulate the blood's pH levels and neutralize acidity. Part of the same family as fennel and parsley, it gives drinks a slightly salty taste. It can be hard to break down its stringiness, even in a powerful blender, but it is great for juicing.

Chard

This leafy vegetable comes in an array of different varieties (rainbow, Swiss, red, golden, and white). This dense vegetable is great to blend. Full of vitamins A, C, and K, it is known to regulate blood sugar levels and provide anti-inflammatory benefits due to its high phytonutrient content.

Dandelion greens

Rich in vitamins A and K, dandelion greens are known to have a purifying effect on the blood and liver. These rather bitter greens are best combined in juices and smoothies with other green vegetables or sweet fruits.

Green pepper

Juicy, crunchy green peppers are silicone-rich and have been shown to improve skin complexion. This vegetable is also a great source of potassium, which balances the fluids and minerals in your body to regulate blood pressure.

Kale

Another member of the cruciferous family, kale is a powerful weapon against bladder, breast, colon, ovarian, and prostate cancer. It is rich in omega-3 fatty acids, treating arthritis and calming inflammation. With more calcium per calorie than milk, kale is great for healthy bones. The waxy, textured variety can be tough, so keep blending until the chunks go away.

Cilantro

This powerful natural cleansing agent has chemical compounds that bind with toxic metals and loosens them from the tissue. This fragrant herb also contains anti-anxiety properties, relieves intestinal gas, aids digestion, calms inflammation, and lowers blood sugar and LDL cholesterol.

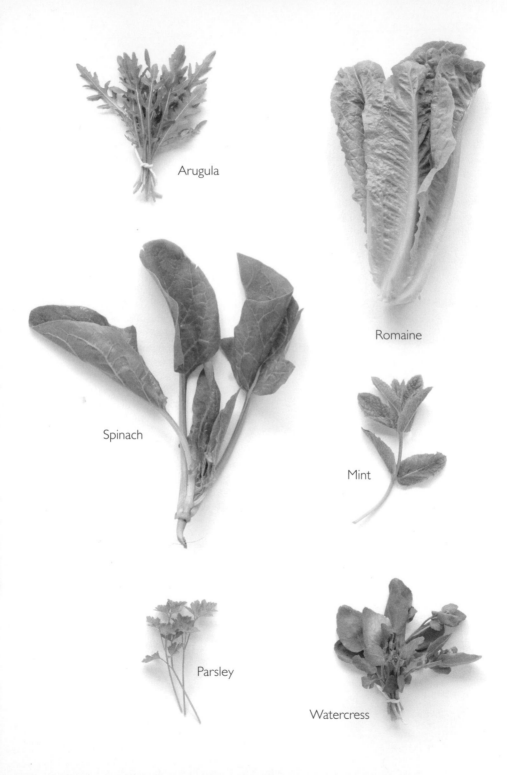

Arugula

Romaine

Spinach

Mint

Parsley

Watercress

Arugula

This peppery salad leaf has a flavor reminiscent of mustard. It is part of the cruciferous family of vegetables, making it a potent anticancer food. It is also a natural aphrodisiac, aids digestion, clears the mind, and is rich in calcium, vitamins A, C, and K, and potassium.

Spinach

Spinach is mild in flavor and rich in vitamins, including A, C, B-2, B-6, E, manganese, folate, magnesium, iron, calcium, and potassium. But it does contain oxalic acid, which can combine with metals in the body and irritate the kidneys, so don't use it in every drink. Spinach helps the digestive system, promotes healthy skin and bones, and also staves off hunger to aid weight loss.

Parsley

This common herb can neutralize some carcinogens and is a great source of folic acid. It promotes carbohydrate metabolism, aiding weight loss, and detoxing the body. It can be stored in your refrigerator for several days after picking and is good at bringing out other flavors in smoothies, such as tomato and celery.

Romaine

Nourish your adrenal cortex with romaine lettuce! This nutritious green leaf lettuce keeps your body in balance and supports your body's natural detoxification process. High in fiber, romaine will clean your digestive tract and strengthen your muscles and heart. It's a great ingredient to add to any smoothie.

Mint

Giving any drink a burst of refreshment, mint helps relax the body and mind. Calming inflammation and digestion, it also has been known to lessen headaches and nausea and alleviate mental stress.

Watercress

Spicy watercress contains vitamins A and C and beta-carotene and has been known to reduce DNA damage in white blood cells. It is also a great green to add to your smoothies to pick things up a bit and to get the blood pumping in your body.

TIPS FOR A JUICE DETOX

We spend an enormous amount of energy on the constant strain of digestion. When we stop eating solid food, all that blood and energy is free to move to the brain, the skin, the liver, and elsewhere, giving our bodies a vacation, allowing it to turn to neglected issues, removing toxins, and ultimately having a rest. With the plan on page 18, you are also flooding yourself all the while with over eleven pounds of raw organic produce.

Please do not try this detox plan if you are under sixteen, pregnant or breast feeding, have any existing health conditions, or use prescription drugs. Always consult your doctor first if you're in doubt.

BEFORE

When you decide to do a detox plan and give your body the vacation it needs, help yourself by cutting out some things a few days before, notably caffeine, alcohol, nicotine, refined sugar, animal products, and wheat. If you spend a few days eating raw foods, broths, juices, and smoothies and drinking lots of water, it will lead to a more comfortable cleanse.

DURING

Try drinking the juices at least every one to two hours so your body has a constant drip of nutrients. Continue to drink water or herbal teas. It's also a good idea to keep warm, as you may feel a little cooler while detoxing. Give yourself time and space to rest, as your body will need this for all the healing that is going on below the surface. Once you have gone through the first big detox days and are drenched in live nutrients, you will experience a sharp clarity, a grounded calm, a sense of weightlessness, and a natural high from within. Sleep will come easily and be deep, rising will feel effortless, and the days in between will flow. You will be charged on revived excitement and stamina. Your skin will glow, your eyes will shine, your body's weight will balance, and you will be buzzing with health.

AFTER

Coming off the detox plan properly is important. On the first day, it is best to just reintroduce soups and smoothies. In the few days following the detox, avoid the same items that you did before the plan and introduce them slowly back into your diet.

SEVEN-DAY GREEN JUICE DETOX PLAN

This plan shows how much juice and smoothie you should consume each day. The juices make up to 10 ounces and the smoothies make up to 24 ounces, depending on how much water you add when blending to your desired consistency. This plan is very easy to use—you drink one recipe quantity of a juice and one recipe quantity of a smoothie each day. You can make each day's drinks in the morning and store them in the refrigerator until you're ready to drink them.

1   DAY ONE

Summer Fresh Juice (page 32)
Strawberry Joy Smoothie (page 72)

BREAKFAST   10 ounces Summer Fresh Juice
MIDMORNING   5 ounces Strawberry Joy Smoothie
LUNCH   7 ounces Strawberry Joy Smoothie
MIDAFTERNOON   5 ounces Strawberry Joy Smoothie
DINNER   7 ounces Strawberry Joy Smoothie

2   DAY TWO

Green Fiber Juice (page 28)
Alkaliner Smoothie (page 86)
+ **Ginger Shot** (page 144)

BREAKFAST   10 ounces Green Fiber Juice
MIDMORNING   5 ounces Alkaliner Smoothie
LUNCH   7 ounces Alkaliner Smoothie
MIDAFTERNOON   5 ounces Alkaliner Smoothie
DINNER   7 ounces Alkaliner Smoothie

Extra shot when you feel like it: Ginger

3   DAY THREE

Green Rocket Tonic (page 22)
Watermelon Smoothie (page 114)

BREAKFAST   10 ounces Green Rocket Tonic
MIDMORNING   5 ounces Watermelon Smoothie
LUNCH   7 ounces Watermelon Smoothie
MIDAFTERNOON   5 ounces Watermelon Smoothie
DINNER   7 ounces Watermelon Smoothie

4 DAY FOUR

Dandelion Tonic (page 24)
Goji Tangerine Smoothie (page 124)

BREAKFAST	10 ounces Dandelion Tonic
MIDMORNING	5 ounces Goji Tangerine Smoothie
LUNCH	7 ounces Goji Tangerine Smoothie
MIDAFTERNOON	5 ounces Goji Tangerine Smoothie
DINNER	7 ounces Goji Tangerine Smoothie

5 DAY FIVE

Grass Energy Juice (page 30)
Avocado Smoothie (page 92)
+ Almond Milk (page 150)

BREAKFAST	10 ounces Grass Energy Juice
MIDMORNING	5 ounces Avocado Smoothie
LUNCH	7 ounces Avocado Smoothie
MIDAFTERNOON	5 ounces Avocado Smoothie
DINNER	7 ounces Avocado Smoothie

Extra milk when you feel like it: Almond milk without the agave nectar

6 DAY SIX

Beetroot Beauty Juice (page 36)
Aloe Protector Smoothie (page 122)

BREAKFAST	10 ounces Beetroot Beauty Juice
MIDMORNING	5 ounces Aloe Protector Smoothie
LUNCH	7 ounces Aloe Protector Smoothie
MIDAFTERNOON	5 ounces Aloe Protector Smoothie
DINNER	7 ounces Aloe Protector Smoothie

7 DAY SEVEN

Cleanser Juice (page 64)
Blueberry Chia Smoothie (page 134)

BREAKFAST	10 ounces Cleanser Juice
MIDMORNING	5 ounces Blueberry Chia Smoothie
LUNCH	7 ounces Blueberry Chia Smoothie
MIDAFTERNOON	5 ounces Blueberry Chia Smoothie
DINNER	7 ounces Blueberry Chia Smoothie

JUICES

Juicing is very quick and easy. All you need is a sharp knife and a cutting board. Remember to peel your citrus fruits if your juicer doesn't have a citrus juicing attachment. Also, make sure that the container you use is under the right spout. Most of these recipes produce 7 to 10 ounces.

GREEN ROCKET TONIC

Savory spice

INGREDIENTS

⅔ cup coconut water • 2 handfuls arugula

1 red apple • A small bunch of cilantro

1 jalapeño (or adjust according to taste)

Pour the coconut water into a glass. Juice all the other
ingredients and add to the glass. Stir, then drink.

This juice is a natural aphrodisiac; it also aids digestion and helps clear the mind.

De *Detoxifying*   **I** *Immunizing*   **BS** *Body Stimulating*

DANDELION TONIC

Savory spice

INGREDIENTS

A pinch of cayenne pepper • ¼ head radicchio

A handful of dandelion greens

A thumb of ginger • A squeeze of lemon

Add the cayenne pepper to the glass. Juice the radicchio, dandelion greens, and ginger and add to the glass. Slice the lemon and squeeze into the glass. Give the juice a little stir, and drink.

This juice is rich in chlorophyll, which helps clean your
vital organs as well as giving your skin a boost.

C *Cleansing* **Di** *Diuretic* **MB** *Metabolism Boosting*

INSALATA
Savory

INGREDIENTS
1 green pepper • 1 beet • 2 celery stalks
3 radishes • ½ cucumber
1 tablespoon olive oil • Juice of 1 lemon

Juice all the vegetables together.
Add the olive oil and lemon juice to the glass and stir.

This juice will not only boost your metabolism, but it is also high in potassium, which helps lower your blood pressure.

I *Immunizing* **BS** *Body Stimulating* **A** *Alkalizing*

GREEN GIANT

Savory

INGREDIENTS

½ head broccoli • A small bunch of green grapes

A handful of spinach • ¼ green cabbage

1 red apple

Juice all the ingredients together.

This juice contains a large amount of vitamin C and is loaded with antioxidants to fight off disease.

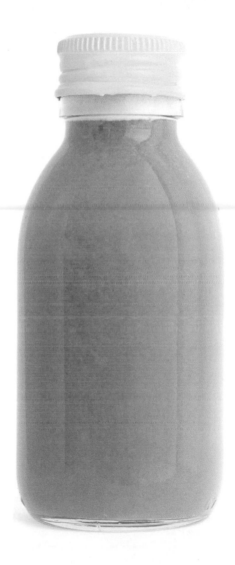 *Digestion Enhancing* **SE** *Skin Enhancing* **BN** *Blood Nourishing*

GRASS ENERGY

Savory . . . only just!

INGREDIENTS

2 handfuls arugula

2 handfuls wheatgrass

2 oranges, peeled

Juice all the ingredients together.

High in vitamins A, C, and K, this juice is an effective stimulant, providing amazing energy and power for the whole body.

MB *Metabolism Boosting* **I** *Immunizing* **BN** *Blood Nourishing*

SUMMER FRESH

Savory and thirst quenching

INGREDIENTS

2 sprigs basil • 2 sprigs mint • 2 handfuls spinach
½ cucumber • ½ lemon, peeled • ½ lime, peeled
A thumb of ginger • 1 red apple (optional)

Juice all the ingredients, adding a red apple if you find it too sour.

This is a delicious juice, rich in vitamins A and K.

A *Alkalizing*   **I** *Immunizing*   **SE** *Skin Enhancing*

GREEN PEPPER
Savory spice

INGREDIENTS
3 jalapeños • 1 green pepper
½ cucumber • 2 handfuls arugula
1 red apple

Juice all the ingredients together.

This juice is full of immune-boosting nutrients and is rich in calcium, vitamin C, and iron.

 *Metabolism Boosting*  *Anti-inflammatory*  *Blood Nourishing*

BEETROOT BEAUTY

Slightly sweet

INGREDIENTS

1 pomegranate • 2 beets

A bunch of red grapes

A squeeze of lemon

Extract the seeds from the pomegranate and juice.
Juice the rest of the ingredients except the lemon. Squeeze the lemon
into the glass, stir all ingredients together, and then drink.

Half of your recommended daily intake of vitamin C
is packed into this juice.

FF *Fat Flushing* **De** *Detoxifying* **SC** *Skin Cleansing*

HEALER
Savory

INGREDIENTS
¼ radicchio • 6 radishes
1 red apple • A small bunch of chard
½ lime, peeled • 2 carrots

Juice all the ingredients together.

38

This invigorating juice is great for the skin and the brain
and is rich in riboflavin and vitamin B-6.

I Immunizing   AO Anti-oxidizing   A Alkalizing

ENERGIZER
Earthy

INGREDIENTS

A handful of kale • 2 handfuls watercress

1 beet • A thumb of ginger • 2 small carrots

A handful of spinach • 1 red apple • 1 orange, peeled

Juice all the ingredients together.

This juice is full of vitamins and minerals, including
high quantities of folic acid.

MBB *Muscle & Bone Building*　**C** *Cleansing*　**I** *Immunizing*

BRUSSELS

Slightly sweet

INGREDIENTS

A handful of brussels sprouts

2 handfuls strawberries

½ butter lettuce

1 orange, peeled

Juice all the ingredients together.

High in vitamin C, this juice helps you stave off hunger.

DE *Digestion Enhancing* **AI** *Anti-inflammatory* **C** *Cleansing*

BRAIN JUICE

Slightly sweet

INGREDIENTS

2 handfuls watercress

½ lime, peeled • ½ lemon, peeled • 2 pears

2 nectarines • 1 teaspoon spirulina powder

Juice all the ingredients except the spirulina. Put the spirulina in a glass,
then stir in the juice slowly so the powder combines well with the juice.

This juice is not only great for your brain, but it also contains a high quantity of vitamin B-12, which is essential for healthy nerves and tissues. Spirulina is found in most health food stores and online.

MB *Metabolism Boosting* **A** *Alkalizing* **AO** *Anti-oxidizing*

POPEYE'S JUICE

Slightly sweet

INGREDIENTS
2 handfuls spinach

⅓ pineapple

2 handfuls raspberries

Juice all the ingredients together.

This juice is high in vitamins and minerals and also gives you a fantastic iron boost.

MB *Metabolism Boosting* **SE** *Skin Enhancing* **DE** *Digestion Enhancing*

FAT BURNER
Savory

INGREDIENTS

3 carrots

A handful of kale

½ lemon, peeled • 2 thumbs ginger

Juice all the ingredients together.

This stimulating juice gets the blood pumping around your body, fighting off any infections in its way.

MB *Metabolism Boosting* **MBB** *Muscle & Bone Building* **I** *Immunizing*

DIGESTIVO
Earthy

INGREDIENTS
2 papayas • 2 handfuls kale
1 pear • 2 sprigs mint
1 lime, peeled

Juice all the ingredients together.

This juice helps to replenish your vitamin C and also has
a calming effect on the body.

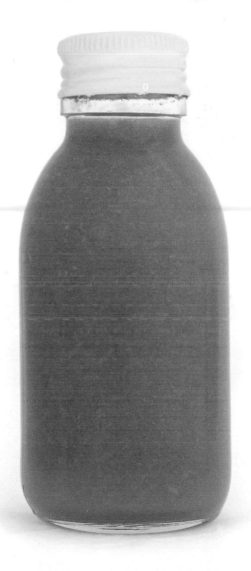 **BN** *Blood Nourishing* **DE** *Digestion Enhancing* **AI** *Anti-inflammatory*

TOMATO LOVER
Savory

INGREDIENTS
2 tomatoes • ½ cucumber
1 bulb fennel • 1 red apple
A small bunch of parsley

———————

Juice all the ingredients together.

This juice contains lots of lycopene, which is great for your heart.

SE *Skin Enhancing* **De** *Detoxifying* **I** *Immunizing*

BERRY INFECTIOUS
Sweet

INGREDIENTS
2 handfuls blueberries
2 handfuls blackcurrants
2 sprigs basil • 2 beets

Juice all the ingredients together.

Packed with antioxidants, this juice is great for your blood.

BN *Blood Nourishing*   **AI** *Anti-inflammatory*   **DE** *Digestion Enhancing*

RASPBERRY MINT

Sweet

INGREDIENTS

2 handfuls raspberries • ½ lime, peeled

2 sprigs mint • 1 peach

2 handfuls spinach

———————

Juice all the ingredients together.

High in vitamin C and antioxidants, this juice
is great for overall health.

BS *Body Stimulating* **C** *Cleansing* **DE** *Digestion Enhancing*

STRAWBERRY

A little sweet

INGREDIENTS

4 handfuls strawberries

2 tomatoes

½ green cabbage

Juice all the ingredients together.

This juice helps boost your cardiovascular health and is an excellent source of vitamin C.

FF *Fat Flushing* **BN** *Blood Nourishing* **I** *Immunizing*

DETOXIFIER
A little sweet

INGREDIENTS
¼ green cabbage • 1 red apple
2 celery stalks
¼ honeydew melon

Juice all the ingredients together.

This juice is a great cleanser for your liver and
is rich in vitamins C and K.

 Skin Enhancing  Muscle & Bone Building  Body Stimulating

CARROT-ENE HEALER

A little sweet

INGREDIENTS
4 carrots

1 red apple

1 sweet potato

Juice all the ingredients together.

A boost for all your organs as well as your skin, this juice is rich in beta-carotene and vitamin A.

I *Immunizing* **BP** *Brain Powering* **SE** *Skin Enhancing*

CLEANSER

Savory

INGREDIENTS
1 celery stalk • A small bunch of parsley

A handful of kale • ½ small head broccoli

A small bunch of dandelion greens • ¼ cantaloupe • 1 kiwi

Juice all the ingredients together.

High in potassium and calcium, this is one of the
best juices you can make.

SE *Skin Enhancing* **DE** *Digestion Enhancing* **BS** *Body Stimulating*

FENNEL
Earthy

INGREDIENTS
1 fennel bulb

¼ red cabbage

4 red apples

Juice all the ingredients together.

This juice is rich in vitamin C and also helps to reduce inflammation.

De *Detoxifying* BN *Blood Nourishing* DE *Digestion Enhancing*

PURPLE GINGER

Sweet

INGREDIENTS

1 beet

2 oranges, peeled

A thumb of ginger

Juice all the ingredients together.

A great juice to drink before you exercise, this helps the
uptake of oxygen in blood cells.

MB *Metabolism Boosting* **BS** *Body Stimulating* **BN** *Blood Nourishing*

SMOOTHIES

Smoothies are really simple to make. You can make them in vast quantities and keep them in the refrigerator for a few days. Most of these smoothies make about 17 ounces with 3 ounces of water added. You can add as much water as you like to the smoothie to achieve your preferred consistency. Some smoothies are much thicker than others, so you will have to add more or less depending on the ingredients used. It all depends on how you like it.

When lemons, oranges, and limes are listed in the ingredients, you should peel them and then blend the whole fruit unless the recipe specifies that you should juice them first.

STRAWBERRY JOY

Sweet

INGREDIENTS
2 bok choy • 2 handfuls strawberries

A small bunch of red grapes

1 banana

Blend the ingredients with ⅓ cup of water. Add more water if necessary,
to reach your desired consistency, then drink.

This smoothie contains lots of vitamin K, which helps build strong bones and reduce inflammation.

 *Anti-oxidizing*  *Fat Flushing*  *Digestion Enhancing*

SMOOTH SPINACH BERRY

Sweet

INGREDIENTS

2 handfuls spinach

A handful of raspberries

A handful of blueberries • 2 oranges, peeled

Blend the ingredients with ⅓ cup of water. Add more water if necessary
to reach your desired consistency, then drink.

This is a smoothie full of vitamins and lots of iron,
which helps to fight urinary infections.

 **BN** *Blood Nourishing* **SE** *Skin Enhancing* **C** *Cleansing*

BANANA TONIC

Slightly sweet

INGREDIENTS

1 romaine lettuce

1 banana

A handful of mint leaves

Blend the ingredients with ⅓ cup of water. Add more water if necessary
to reach your desired consistency, then drink.

This smoothie helps give your body a sense of calm and is a good source of vitamin B-6, vitamin C, and potassium.

D *Diuretic* *BN* *Blood Nourishing* *AI* *Anti-inflammatory*

TROPICAL CABBAGE
Sweet

INGREDIENTS
½ green cabbage • Flesh of ⅓ pineapple
Flesh of 2 mangoes • A thumb of ginger
1 teaspoon honey

Blend the ingredients except the honey with ⅓ cup of water. Add more water if necessary to reach your desired consistency. Add the honey, mix, then drink.

Rich in vitamins C and K, this smoothie also aids digestion.

MB *Metabolism Boosting* DE *Digestion Enhancing* SE *Skin Enhancing*

COCONUT KALE

Sweet

INGREDIENTS

2 handfuls kale • 1 banana • Flesh of ⅓ pineapple

2 tablespoons grated coconut meat

⅔ cup coconut water

Blend the ingredients with ⅓ cup of water. Add more water if necessary
to reach your desired consistency, then drink.

Rich in vitamins A, C, and K, this is a great antibacterial smoothie.

I Immunizing FF Fat Flushing MBB Muscle & Bone Building

HEARTY PEAR
Slightly sweet

INGREDIENTS
A handful of kale • 1 bok choy
2 pears • A handful of strawberries
A squeeze of lime

Blend the ingredients with ⅓ cup of water. Add more water if necessary
to reach your desired consistency, then drink.

High in antioxidants, this smoothie is also great for your eyes.

DE *Digestion Enhancing* **I** *Immunizing* **BN** *Blood Nourishing*

HIGH ON FIBER
Slightly sweet

INGREDIENTS
1 romaine lettuce • 1 bok choy
5 apricots • A handful of blueberries
1 banana • A small bunch of green grapes

Blend the ingredients with ⅓ cup of water. Add more water if necessary
to reach your desired consistency, then drink.

Rich in vitamins C and K, this smoothie is great
for your digestive system.

C Cleansing BN Blood Nourishing De Detoxifying

ALKALINER

Slightly sweet

INGREDIENTS
2 handfuls kale • 2 sprigs mint
1 orange, peeled • ½ lemon, peeled

Blend the ingredients with ⅓ cup of water. Add more water if necessary
to reach your desired consistency, then drink.

This smoothie is known to be a good stress reliever
and is rich in vitamins A, C, and K.

 **AI** *Anti-inflammatory* **BN** *Blood Nourishing* **D** *Diuretic*

BLUEBERRY KALE

Slightly sweet

INGREDIENTS

2 handfuls kale

2 handfuls blueberries

2 pears • Juice of ½ lemon

Blend the ingredients with ⅓ cup of water. Add more water if necessary
to reach your desired consistency, then drink.

Full of vitamins A, C, and K, this smoothie is good
for enriching your blood.

 *Anti-inflammatory*  *Muscle & Bone Building*  *Digestion Enhancing*

PEACHY
Slightly sweet

INGREDIENTS

2 handfuls spinach • 2 peaches

½ handful of mint leaves

1 tablespoon honey

Blend the ingredients except the honey with ⅓ cup of water.
Add more water if necessary to reach your desired consistency.
Add the honey, mix, and then drink.

Peaches are great at helping you feel full as well as being packed with vitamin C, vitamin A, and potassium.

BS *Body Stimulating*   **BN** *Blood Nourishing*   **MBB** *Muscle & Bone Building*

AVOCADO
Slightly savory

INGREDIENTS

1 avocado • A small handful of parsley leaves

½ cucumber • 2 sprigs dill

Juice of ½ lemon

Blend the ingredients with ⅓ cup of water. Add more water if necessary
to reach your desired consistency, then drink.

This smoothie, which is high in chlorophyll,
is great at cleansing your vital organs.

BN *Blood Nourishing* **AI** *Anti-inflammatory* **C** *Cleansing*

TOMATO BASIL
Savory

INGREDIENTS
2 tomatoes • A sprig of basil

2 celery stalks • 2 handfuls spinach

A squeeze of lemon

Blend the ingredients with ⅓ cup of water. Add more water if necessary
to reach your desired consistency, then drink.

Tomatoes are known to help lower your risk of cancer because they are full of antioxidants.

 *Skin Enhancing* *Cleansing* *Body Stimulating*

CILANTRO PEPPER

Savory spice

INGREDIENTS

A handful of cilantro leaves • 1 bok choy • 1 red apple
2 celery stalks • A thumb of ginger • A pinch of turmeric
A pinch of cayenne pepper • A squeeze of lemon

Blend the ingredients with ⅓ cup of water. Add more water if necessary
to reach your desired consistency, then drink.

This smoothie is high in iron and great at combating
various digestive ailments.

 *Metabolism Boosting*  *Blood Nourishing*  *Immunizing*

JALAPEÑO HEALER

Savory spice

INGREDIENTS

3 slices pickled jalapeño

A small handful of cilantro leaves • A handful of kale

A thumb of ginger • 1 clove garlic • 2 oranges, peeled

Blend the ingredients with ⅓ cup of water. Add more water if necessary
to reach your desired consistency, then drink.

This smoothie has great healing properties and
is high in vitamins A, C, and K.

 Anti-inflammatory  Blood Nourishing  Alkalizing

FENNEL BREEZE

Savory

INGREDIENTS

1 fennel bulb • 2 sprigs oregano • 2 sprigs basil
2 handfuls kale • ½ cucumber • 1 tomato
½ avocado • A squeeze of lime

Blend the ingredients with ⅓ cup of water. Add more water if necessary
to reach your desired consistency, then drink.

Treat your skin by drinking this smoothie,
which is rich in vitamin C and fiber.

De *Detoxifying* **BN** *Blood Nourishing* **DE** *Digestion Enhancing*

MORNING KICKSTART
Savory

INGREDIENTS
2 handfuls watercress • 1 tablespoon wheat germ
1 tablespoon flaxseed • Juice of 1 lemon • Honey (optional)

Blend the ingredients with ⅓ cup of water. Add more water if necessary
to reach your desired consistency. Add honey, to taste if you like
a little sweetness, mix, then drink.

This body-boosting smoothie brightens up every cell in your body and is rich in vitamin A, vitamin K, and calcium.

BS *Body Stimulating* **BN** *Blood Nourishing* **FF** *Fat Flushing*

FRUIT AND FIBER

Slightly sweet

INGREDIENTS

A big bunch of cilantro

2 handfuls strawberries

⅔ cup coconut water • 1 banana

Blend the ingredients with ⅓ cup of water. Add more water if necessary
to reach your desired consistency, then drink.

This smoothie helps to reduce cholesterol and is rich in fiber.

 *Detoxifying*  *Fat Flushing*  *Body Stimulating*

VANILLA AND FIGS
Slightly sweet

INGREDIENTS
4 small figs or 2 large ones • 2 handfuls spinach
2 peaches • A pinch of cinnamon
2 drops vanilla extract

Blend the ingredients with ⅓ cup of water. Add more water if necessary
to reach your desired consistency, then drink.

Rich in fiber and potassium, this is a great calming smoothie
for those who suffer from anxiety.

 *Blood Nourishing*  *Muscle & Bone Building*  *Body Stimulating*

PINEAPPLE TWIST

Slightly sweet

INGREDIENTS

Flesh of ⅓ pineapple

A small handful of cilantro

1 banana • 2 sprigs mint

Blend the ingredients with ⅓ cup of water. Add more water if necessary
to reach your desired consistency, then drink.

Rich in vitamin C, this smoothie helps aid digestion.

DE *Digestion Enhancing* **AI** *Anti-inflammatory* **De** *Detoxifying*

NECTARINE SOUR

Bittersweet

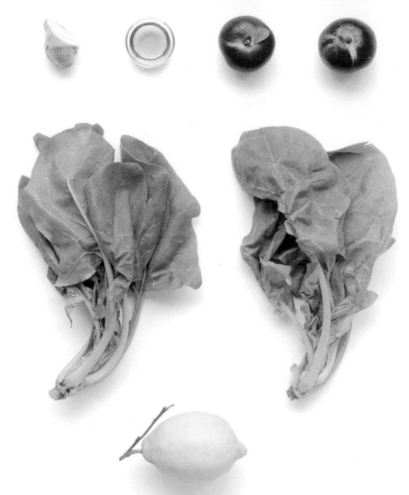

INGREDIENTS

2 handfuls spinach • 2 nectarines

A thumb of ginger • 1 tablespoon honey

1 whole lemon, including peel and pith

Blend the ingredients with ⅓ cup of water. Add more water if necessary
to reach your desired consistency, then drink.

This smoothie helps prevent allergies and
is full of vitamins and iron.

Di *Diuretic* **A** *Alkalizing* **AI** *Anti-inflammatory*

KING OF THE FRUITS

Slightly sweet

INGREDIENTS

2 handfuls kale

Flesh of 3 large mangoes

1 teaspoon chia seeds

Blend the ingredients with at least ⅓ cup of water. The chia seeds thicken this smoothie, so add enough water to reach your desired consistency.

This smoothie will give you a big boost of vitamins A, C, and K.
Chia seeds can be bought from most health food stores and online.

 *Body Stimulating*  *Blood Nourishing*  *Alkalizing*

WATERMELON

Slightly sweet

INGREDIENTS

Flesh of ¾ small watermelon or ¼ large watermelon, seeds removed

1 romaine lettuce • 1 banana

A squeeze of lemon

Blend the ingredients except the lemon with ⅓ cup of water.
Add more water if necessary to reach your desired consistency.
Add a squeeze of lemon, mix, then drink.

Rich in lycopene, this smoothie is great for flushing out
your kidneys and bladder.

Anti-oxidizing *Immunizing* *Diuretic*

GREEN PAPAYA

Slightly sweet

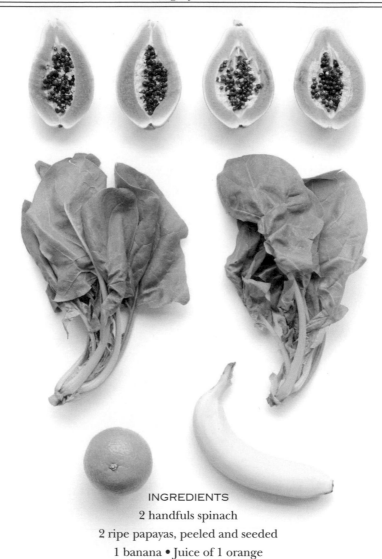

INGREDIENTS

2 handfuls spinach

2 ripe papayas, peeled and seeded

1 banana • Juice of 1 orange

Blend the spinach, papayas, banana, and ⅓ cup of water.
Add the orange juice to the smoothie. Add more water until it
reaches your desired consistency, mix, and drink.

Rich in vitamin C and iron, this juice also
helps you fight cancer.

I *Immunizing* **SE** *Skin Enhancing* **C** *Cleansing*

SUPER CANTALOUPE

Slightly sweet

INGREDIENTS

1 romaine lettuce

Flesh of 1 cantaloupe

A sprig of mint

Blend the ingredients with ⅓ cup of water. Add more water if necessary
to reach your desired consistency, then drink.

Rich in vitamins A and K, this smoothie is a powerful cleanser, and also helps with anxiety.

 *Blood Nourishing*  *Anti-inflammatory*  *Diuretic*

BLACKCURRANT

Sweet

INGREDIENTS

A handful of blackcurrants

Flesh of 1 mango • 1 butter lettuce

1 orange, peeled

Blend the ingredients with ⅓ cup of water. Add more water if necessary
to reach your desired consistency, then drink.

Packed with vitamin A, vitamin B-6, and potassium, this smoothie can also help with urinary infections.

I *Immunizing* **BS** *Body Stimulating* **BP** *Brain Powering*

ALOE PROTECTOR

Slightly sweet

INGREDIENTS

1 tablespoon aloe vera juice

A small bunch of red grapes

1 red leaf lettuce • Flesh of 1 kiwi • 1 orange, peeled

Blend the ingredients with ⅓ cup of water. Add more water if necessary
to reach your desired consistency, then drink.

High in vitamin C, this smoothie also helps improve your blood circulation. Aloe vera juice can be found in most health food stores or online.

SE *Skin Enhancing* **De** *Detoxifying* **DE** *Digestion Enhancing*

GOJI TANGERINE

Slightly sweet

INGREDIENTS

2 teaspoons dried goji berries

Flesh of 1 mango • 1 tangerine, peeled

2 celery stalks • 1 butter lettuce

Blend the ingredients with ⅓ cup of water. Add more water if necessary
to reach your desired consistency, and drink.

This smoothie is packed with vitamin C and beta-carotene, which enhances your skin and reduces inflammation. Goji berries can be found in supermarkets, health food stores, or online.

BP *Brain Powering* **AI** *Anti-inflammatory* **SE** *Skin Enhancing*

CINNAMON-DATE DIGESTIVE

Slightly sweet

INGREDIENTS

1 romaine lettuce • 2 red apples

4 dates, pitted • A pinch of ground cinnamon

1 orange, peeled

Blend the ingredients with ⅓ cup of water. Add more water if necessary
to reach your desired consistency, then drink.

This smoothie helps lower your cholesterol as well
as being full of vitamins A, K, and C.

BN *Blood Nourishing* **FF** *Fat Flushing* **DE** *Digestion Enhancing*

LEEK AND CUCUMBER

Savory

INGREDIENTS

1 leek • ½ cucumber • ½ avocado

5 radishes • 1 clove garlic

½ lemon, peeled • Sliced jalapeño (optional)

Blend the ingredients with ⅓ cup of water. If you like a bit of spice, add a few slices of jalapeño. Add more water if necessary to reach your desired consistency, then drink.

Rich in kaempferol and folate, this smoothie helps cleanse your body of toxins.

SE *Skin Enhancing* **DE** *Digestion Enhancing* **BS** *Body Stimulating*

WATERCRESS

Slightly sweet

INGREDIENTS

2 handfuls watercress

1 orange, peeled • 1 avocado

½ lime, peeled

Blend the ingredients with ⅓ cup of water. Add more water if necessary
to reach your desired consistency, then drink.

This smoothie is full of vitamins A, C, and K, and can also help to alleviate early signs of a headache.

 Blood Nourishing    Skin Enhancing    Alkalizing

SKIN TONIC

Slightly sweet

INGREDIENTS

½ avocado • ½ bunch asparagus

2 oranges, peeled • A sprig of basil

A squeeze of lemon

Blend the ingredients with ⅓ cup of water. Add more water if necessary
to reach your desired consistency, then drink.

This smoothie enhances your beauty from within
because it's high in nutrients and fiber.

 Body Stimulating  Blood Nourishing  Skin Enhancing

BLUEBERRY CHIA

Slightly sweet

INGREDIENTS

2 handfuls blueberries
1 orange, peeled • 1 tablespoon chia seeds
½ head broccoli

Blend the ingredients with ⅓ cup of water. Add more water if necessary
to reach your desired consistency, then drink.

This juice is a natural aphrodisiac, aids digestion, and helps clear the mind. Chia seeds can be bought from most health food stores and online.

 *Anti-inflammatory* SE *Skin Enhancing* MB *Metabolism Boosting*

SHOTS AND MILKS

Shots are great for when you feel like you need a healthy boost. Add them to your juices or smoothies, or drink them alone for a quick pick-me-up.

Milks are also highly nutritious and can be added to your smoothies or juices or enjoyed on their own. Nuts are high in monounsaturated fats, which help keep our hearts healthy and disease free. They are also a great source of protein, minerals, and other life-enhancing nutrients.

A natural sweetener is added to most of the milks, and can be adjusted according to taste. Popular natural sweeteners include agave nectar, honey, and real maple syrup. All milks can been stored in the refrigerator for up to three days.

ALOE

Slightly sweet

INGREDIENTS

1 teaspoon aloe vera juice

1 green apple, juiced

Pour the aloe vera juice into a glass, then add the juiced apple.

This shot helps lower cholesterol and blood sugar.
Aloe vera juice can be found in most health food stores or online.

BN *Blood Nourishing*   **DE** *Digestion Enhancing*

GREEN WITH ENVY

Savory

INGREDIENTS

1 teaspoon spirulina powder

1 green apple, juiced

A squeeze of lemon

Put the spirulina into a glass, then juice the apple with the squeeze
of lemon and add to the glass. Combine well.

This shot is high in protein and minerals.
Spirulina is found in most health food stores and online.

BS *Body Stimulating* **C** *Cleansing*

FLU KICK

Savory spice

INGREDIENTS

1 teaspoon agave nectar • A pinch of cayenne pepper
½ clove garlic • ½ thumb ginger
½ orange • ½ lemon

Put the agave syrup into a glass and add the cayenne. Juice the garlic, ginger, orange, and lemon, then pour into the glass.

This shot is not for the faint-hearted! It provides a boost to your blood and will help to fight symptoms of the flu.

I *Immunizing* **BS** *Body Stimulating*

GINGER

Savory

INGREDIENTS

1 teaspoon agave nectar

½ lemon

2 thumbs ginger

Put the agave nectar into a glass, then juice the lemon and ginger
and add to the glass. Combine well.

This shot is good for your respiratory system as well as your heart.

DE *Digestion Enhancing* BN *Blood Nourishing*

BRAZIL NUT MILK

Slightly sweet

INGREDIENTS

5 ounces Brazil nuts • 2 tablespoons coconut oil

2 tablespoons agave nectar

1 teaspoon vanilla • A pinch of sea salt

2½ cups water

Fully cover the Brazil nuts in water and soak for up to 6 hours to obtain the best flavor. Dry the nuts before you start.

Using fresh water, place all of the ingredients into a blender and blend for at least 1 minute. For the best results, strain through cheesecloth or a piece of muslin, using the back of a ladle to push through as much liquid as possible.

This special milk is full of fiber, selenium, and vitamin E.

BN *Blood Nourishing*   I *Immunizing*   BS *Body Stimulating*

PINE NUT MILK

Rich and sweet

INGREDIENTS

2½ ounces pine nuts

2 tablespoons honey

1 cup water

Pine nuts do not need to be pre-soaked.

Place the ingredients in a blender and blend for a good minute.
For the best results, strain through cheesecloth or a piece of muslin, using
the back of a ladle to push through as much liquid as possible.

This is a delicious milk that is rich in vitamin A
and also good for your heart.

 Immunizing  Fat Flushing

ALMOND MILK

Slightly sweet

INGREDIENTS

5 ounces almonds

2 tablespoons coconut oil • 2 tablespoons agave nectar

1 teaspoon vanilla • A pinch of salt

2½ cups water

For the best results, fully cover the almonds in water and soak for 6 to 8 hours.
Drain before using. Using fresh water, blend the ingredients until
smooth and creamy. Strain through cheesecloth or muslin, using the back
of a ladle to push through as much liquid as possible.

This is a great milk for lowering cholesterol.

MBB *Muscle & Bone Building* **AO** *Anti-oxidizing*

PUMPKIN SEED MILK

Slightly sweet

INGREDIENTS

4½ ounces pumpkin seeds

2 dates, pitted • 2 tablespoons honey

A pinch of salt • 2 cups water

Blend all the ingredients together.
Strain through cheesecloth or a piece of muslin, using the back
of a ladle to push through as much liquid as possible.

A rich source of zinc, this milk helps you sleep well
and enhances your mood.

A *Alkalizing* AI *Anti-inflammatory*

CHOCOLATE CASHEW MILK

Slightly sweet

INGREDIENTS

3½ ounces cashew nuts • ⅓ cup cocoa powder
1 tablespoon coconut oil • 2 tablespoons agave nectar
1 teaspoon vanilla • ½ teaspoon salt • 2½ cups water

Fully cover the cashews in water and soak for 30 minutes. Drain before using.
Using fresh water, blend all the ingredients together on high speed. Chill
before serving. If you would like this a little sweeter, just add more agave nectar.

This protein-packed milk is a great mood enhancer.

I *Immunizing* **AI** *Anti-inflammatory* **BN** *Blood Nourishing*

PECAN MILK

Slightly sweet

INGREDIENTS

4 ounces pecans, toasted and unsalted • 3 dates, pitted

2 tablespoons agave nectar • 1½ teaspoons ground cinnamon

½ teaspoon vanilla • 1½ cups water

Fully cover the pecans in water and soak for 6 to 8 hours or overnight for the best results. Drain before using. Using fresh water, place all the ingredients in a blender and blend for at least 1 minute. Chill before drinking.

This milk contains over twenty essential vitamins and minerals.

 *Blood Nourishing*  *Digestion Enhancing*  *Brain Powering*

INDEX

Originally published in French in France as *Green Smoothies: La Bible* by
Marabout, a member of Hachette Livre, Paris, in 2014. This edition was
subsequently published in slightly different form in Australia by Hachette
Australia, an imprint of Hachette Australia Pty. Limited, Sydney, in 2014.

Library of Congress Cataloging-in-Publication Data
Green, Fern, author.
[Green smoothies. English]
Green smoothies / Fern Green. — First American edition.
pages cm
"Originally published in French in France as Green Smoothies: La Bible by
Marabout, a member of Hachette Livre, Paris, in 2014."
Includes index.
1. Smoothies (Beverages)   I. Title.
TX817.S636G7413 2015
641.8'75—dc23
2015026205

Trade Paperback ISBN: 978-1-60774-938-7
eBook ISBN: 978-1-60774-939-4

Printed in China

Design by Helen McTeer
Photography by Deirdre Rooney

10 9 8 7 6 5 4 3

First American Edition